I0011511

Book 1
Windows 8 Tips for Beginners
BY SAM KEY

&

Book 2
Rails Programming Professional Made Easy
BY SAM KEY

Book 1
Windows 8 Tips for Beginners

BY SAM KEY

A Simple, Easy, and Efficient Guide to a Complex System of Windows 8!

Programming Box Set #99: Windows 8 Tips for Beginners & Rails Programming Professional Made Easy

Programming Box Set #99: Windows 8 Tips for Beginners & Rails Programming Professional Made Easy

Table Of Contents

Introduction 5

Chapter 1: How is Windows 8 Different from Previous Versions? 6

Chapter 2: How to Get Started with Windows 8 9

Chapter 3: How to Personalize Your Start Screen 14

Chapter 4: How to Manage Your Files and Folders 17

Chapter 5: How to Get Started with the Desktop 19

Conclusion 22

Introduction

I want to thank you and congratulate you for purchasing the book, "Windows 8 Tips for Beginners: A Simple, easy, and efficient guide to a complex system of windows 8!"

This book contains proven steps and strategies on how to familiarize yourself with the new features of Windows 8 which were designed to make your computing experience simpler and more enjoyable. You will not only learn how to navigate through Windows 8 , but you will also learn how Windows 8 is similar to and different from the older versions so you can easily adjust and take advantage of the benefits that Windows 8 has in store for you.

Thanks again for purchasing this book, I hope you enjoy it!

Chapter 1: How is Windows 8 Different from Previous Versions?

With Windows 8, Microsoft launched a lot of new changes and features, some of which are minor , but others are major. Some of the changes you can see in Windows 8 are the redesigned interface, enhanced security and other online features.

Changes in the Interface

The most glaring change you will observe when you first open your computer with Windows 8 is that the screen looks completely different from older Windows versions. The Windows 8 interface has new features such as Start screen, hot corners, and live tiles.

- The Start screen will be the main screen where you will find all of your installed programs and they will be in the form of "tiles". You can personalize your Start Screen by rearranging the tiles, selecting a background image and changing the color scheme.
- You can navigate through Windows 8 using the "hot corners", which you activate by hovering the mouse pointer over the corners of the screen. For instance, if you want to switch to another open application, hover your mouse in the top-left corner of your screen and then click on the app.
- Certain apps have Live Tile functions, which enable you to see information even if the app itself is not open. For instance, you can easily see the current weather on the Weather app tile from your Start screen; if you want to see more information, you can just click on the app to open it.
- You can now find many of the settings of your computer in the Charms bar that you can open by hovering the mouse in the bottom-right or top-right corner of your computer screen.

Online Features in Windows 8

Because of the ease of accessing Internet now, many people have started to save their documents and other data online. Microsoft has made it easier to save on the cloud through their OneDrive service (this was formerly called SkyDrive). Windows 8 is capable of linking to OneDrive and other online social networks such as Twitter and Facebook in a seamless manner.

To connect your computer to OneDrive, sign in using your free Microsoft account instead of your own computer account. When you do this, all of the contacts, files and other information stored in your OneDrive are all in your Start screen. You can also use another computer to sign in to your Microsoft account and access all of your OneDrive files. You can also easily link your Flickr, Twitter and Facebook accounts to Windows 8 so you will be able to see the updates straight from your Start screen. You can also do this through the People app which is included in Windows 8.

Other Features

- The Desktop is now simpler for enhanced speed. Yes, the Desktop is still included in Windows 8 and you can still manage your documents or open your installed programs through the Desktop. However, with Windows 8, a number of the transparency effects that frequently caused Windows Vista and Windows 7 to slow down are now gone. This allows the Desktop to operate smoother on nearly all computers.

- The Start menu, once considered as a vital feature in previous Windows versions, is now the Start screen. You can now open your installed programs or search for your files through the Start screen. This can be quite disorienting if you are just starting with Windows 8.

- Windows 8 has enhanced security because of its integrated antivirus program referred to as Windows Defender. This antivirus program is also useful in protecting you from different kinds of malware. In addition, it can aid in keeping you and your computer secure by telling you which data each of your installed apps can access. For instance, certain apps can access your location, so if you do not want other people to know where you are, just change your preference in the settings/configuration part of your apps.

How to Use Windows 8

Because Windows 8 is not like the older versions, it will possibly change how you have been using your computer. You may need quite some time to get accustomed to the new features, but you just need to remember that those changes are necessary to enhance your computing experience. For instance, if you have used older Windows versions, you may be used to clicking on the Start button to launch programs. You need to get used to using the Start screen with Windows 8. Of course, you can still use the Desktop view to make file and folder organization easier and to launch older programs.

You may need to switch between the Desktop view and the Start screen to work on your computer. Don't feel bad if you feel disoriented at first because you will get used to it. Moreover, if you just use your computer to surf the internet, you may be spending majority of your time in the Start screen anyway.

Chapter 2: How to Get Started with Windows 8

Windows 8 can truly be bewildering at the start because of the many changes done to the interface. You will need to learn effective navigation of both the Start screen and Desktop view. Even though the Desktop view appears similar to the older Windows versions, it has one major change that you need to get used to – the Start menu is no more.

In this chapter, you will learn how to work with the apps and effectively navigate Windows 8 using the Charms bar. You will learn where to look for the features that you could previously find in the Start menu.

How to Sign In

While setting up Windows 8, you will be required to create your own account name and password that you will use to sign in. You can also opt to create other account names and associate each account name with a specific Microsoft account. You will then see your own user account name and photo (if you have uploaded one). Key in your password and press enter. To select another user, click on the back arrow to choose from the available options. After you have signed in, the Start screen will be displayed.

How to Navigate Windows 8

You can use the following ways to navigate your way through Windows 8

- You can use the hot corners to navigate through Windows 8. You can use them whether you are in the Desktop view or in the Start screen. Simply hover your mouse in the corner of the screen to access the hot corners. You will see a tile or a toolbar that you can then click to open. All the corners perform various tasks. For instance, hovering the pointer on the lower-left corner will return you to the Start screen. The upper-left corner will allow you to switch to the last application that you were using. The lower-right or upper-right corners gives you access to the Charms bar where you can either manage your printers or adjust the settings of your computer. Hover your mouse towards the upper-left corner and then move your mouse down to see the list of the different applications that you are simultaneously using. You can simply on any application to go back to it.

- You can also navigate through Windows 8 through different keyboard shortcuts.
    - Alt+Tab is the most useful shortcut; you use it to switch between open applications in both the Start screen and Desktop view.
    - You can use the Windows key to go back to the Start screen. It also works in both the Desktop view and Start screen.
    - From the Start screen, you can go to the Desktop view by clicking on Windows+D.
- You can access the settings and other features of your computer through the toolbar referred to as Charms bar. Place your mouse pointer on the bottom-right or top-right corner of your screen to display the Charms bar wherein you can see the following icons or "charms":
    - The Search charm allows you to look for files, apps or settings on your computer. However, a simpler method to do a search is through the Start screen wherein you can simply key in the name of the application or file that you want to find.
    - You can think of the Share charm as a "copy and paste" attribute that is included in Windows 8 to make it easier for you to work with your computer. Using the Share charm, you can "copy" data like a web address or a picture from one app and then "paste" it onto another application. For instance, if you are reading a certain article in the Internet, you can share the website address in your Mail application so you can send it to a friend.
    - The Start charm will allow you to go back to the Start screen. If you are currently on the Start screen, the Start charm will launch the latest app that you used.

- The Devices charm displays all of the hardware devices that are linked to your computer such as monitors and printers.
- Through the Settings charm, you can open both the general setting of your computer and the settings of the application that you are presently using. For instance, if you are presently using the web browser, you can access the Internet Options through the Settings charm.

How to Work with the Start Screen Applications

You may need to familiarize yourself with the Start screen applications because they are quite different from the "classic" Windows applications from previous versions. The apps in Windows 8 fill the whole screen rather than launching in a window. However, you can still do multi-tasking by launching two or more applications next to each other.

- To open an application from the Start screen, look for the app that you want to launch and click on it.
- To close an application hover your mouse at the top portion of the application, and you will notice that the cursor will become a hand icon, click and hold your mouse and then drag it towards the bottommost part of the screen and then release. When the app has closed, you will go back to the Start screen.

How to View Apps Side by Side

Even though the applications normally fill up the whole screen, Windows 8 still allows you to snap an application to the right or left side and then launch other applications beside it. For instance, you can work on a word document while viewing the calendar app. Here are the steps to view applications side by side:

1. Go to the Start screen and then click on the first app that you want to open.
2. Once the app is open, click on the title bar and drag the window to the left or right side of your computer screen.

3. Release your mouse and you will see that the application has snapped to the side of your computer screen.

4. You can go back to the Start screen by clicking at any empty space of the computer screen.

5. Click on another application that you want to open.

6. You will now see the applications displayed side by side. You can also adjust the size of the applications by dragging the bar.

Please note that the snapping feature is intended to work with a widescreen monitor. Your minimum screen resolution should be 1366 x 768 pixels to enjoy the snapping feature fully. If your monitor has a bigger screen, you will be able to snap more than two apps simultaneously.

How to cope with the Start menu

Many people have already complained about the missing Start menu in Windows 8. For many Windows users, the Start menu is a very vital feature because they use to open applications, look for files, launch the Control Panel and shut down their computer. You can actually do all of these things in Windows 8 too, but you will now have to look for them in different locations.

- There are a number of ways to launch an application in Windows 8. You can launch an app by clicking the application icon on the taskbar or double-clicking the application shortcut form the Desktop view or clicking the application tile in the Start screen.

- You can look for an app or a file by pressing the Windows key to go back to the Start screen. When you are there, you can simply key in the filename or app name that you want to look for. The results of your search will be immediately displayed underneath the search bar. You will also see a list of recommended web searches underneath the search results.

- You can launch the Control Panel by going to the Desktop view and then hovering your mouse in the lower-right corner of the computer screen to display the Charms bar and then selecting Settings. From the Settings Pane, look for and choose Control Panel.

After the Control Panel pops up, you can start choosing your preferred settings.

- You can shut down your computer by hovering the mouse in the lower-right corner of your screen to display the Charms bar and then selecting Settings. Click on the Power icon and then choose Shut Down.

Start Screen Options

If you prefer to continue working with the Desktop view more often, you actually have a number of alternatives that can let your computer operate more like the older Windows versions. One of these alternatives is the "boot your computer directly to the Desktop" rather than the Start screen. Here are the steps to change your Start screen options:

1. Return to the Desktop view.
2. Right-click the taskbar then choose Properties.
3. You will then see a dialog box where you can choose the options that you want to change.

Chapter 3: How to Personalize Your Start Screen

If you are open to the idea of spending most of your time on the Start screen of your computer, there are different ways you can do to personalize it based on your preferences. You can change the background color and image, rearrange the applications, pin applications and create application groups.

- You can change the background of your Start screen by hovering the mouse in the lower-right corner of your screen to open up the Charms bar and then selecting the Settings icon. Choose Personalize and then choose your preferred color scheme and background image.

- You can change the lock screen picture by displaying the Charms bar again and the selecting the Settings icon. Choose Change PC settings and then choose Lock screen that is located near to the topmost part of the screen. Choose your preferred image from the thumbnail photos shown. You can also opt to click on Browse to choose your own photos. You will see the lock screen every time you return to your computer after leaving it inactive for a set number of minutes. However, you can also manually lock your screen by clicking on your account name and then choosing Lock.

- You can change your own account photo by displaying the Charms bar and then choosing the Settings icon. Click on the Change PC setting and choose Account picture. You can look for your own photos by clicking Browse, will let you browse the folders in your computer. Once you find the picture you want to use, click on Choose image to set it as your account picture. If you are running a laptop, you can also use the built-in webcam to take a picture of yourself for your account photo.

How to Customize the Start Screen Applications

You do not really need to put up with the pre-arranged apps on your Start screen. You can change how they look by rearranging them based on your own preference. You can move an app by clicking, holding and dragging the application to your preferred location. Let go of your mouse and the app tile will automatically move to the new place.

You may also think that the animation in the live tiles is very disturbing while you are working. Do not worry because you can simply turn the animation off so that you will only see a plain background. You can do this by right-clicking the application that you wish to change. A toolbar pop up from the bottom part of your computer screen. Simply choose Turn live tile off and the animation if you don't want real-time notifications.

How to Pin Applications to the Start Screen

By default, you won't be able to see all of the installed applications on the Start screen. However, you can easily "pin" your favorite apps on the Start screen so you can access them easily. You can do this by clicking the arrow found in the bottom-left corner of your Start screen. You will then see the list of all the applications that you have installed. Look for the app you want to pin and the right-click it. You will see Pin to Start at the lowest part of the screen. Click on it to pin your app.

To unpin or remove an application from the Start screen, right-click the app icon you want to remove and then choose "Unpin from Start".

How to Create Application Groups

There are more ways to bring organization to your apps. One way is to create an app group wherein you can similar apps together. You can give a specific name for each app group for easier retrieval. You can create a new application group by clicking, holding and dragging an application to the right side until you see it on an empty space of the Start screen. Let go of your mouse to let the app be inside its own application group. You will be able to see a distinct space between the new app group that you have just created and the other app groups. You can then drag other apps into the new group.

You can name your new application group by right clicking any of the apps on the Start screen and then clicking Name group at the top of the application group. When choosing a group name, opt for shorter, but more descriptive names. After you have keyed in your group name, press the Enter key.

Chapter 4: How to Manage Your Files and Folders

The File Explorer found in the Desktop view is very handy in managing files and folders in your computer. If you are familiar with older Windows version, File Explorer is actually the same as Windows Explorer. You will usually use the File Explorer for opening, accessing and rearranging folders and files in the Desktop view. You can launch the File Explorer by clicking the folder icon found on the taskbar.

The View tab in the File Explorer enables you to alter how the files appear inside the folders. For instance, you may choose to the List view when viewing documents and the Large Icons view when looking at photos. You can change the content view by selecting the View tab and then choosing your preferred view from the Layout group.

For certain folders, you can also sort your files in different ways – by name, size, file type, date modified, date created, among others. You can sort your files by selecting the View tab, clicking on the Sort by button and then choosing your preferred view from the drop-down list.

How to Search Using the File Explorer

Aside from using the Charms bar to look for files, you can also use the Search bar in the File Explorer. Actually, the File Explorer provides search options that are more advanced than those offered by the Charms bar. This is very useful when you are finding it quite hard to look for a particular document.

Every time you key in a word into the search bar, you will see that the Search Tools tab automatically opens on the Ribbon. You can find the advanced search options on the Search Tools tab. You can use them to filter your search by size, file type or date modified. You can also see the latest searches that you have made.

How to Work with Libraries

Windows 8 has 4 main libraries: Documents, Music, Pictures and Videos. Whenever you need a specific file, you can search for them through the Libraries or groups of content that you can readily access via the File Explorer.

The folders and files that you create are not actually stored in the Libraries themselves. The libraries are just there to help you better organize your stuff. You can place your own folders inside the libraries without the need to change their actual location in your computer. For instance, you can place a folder your recent photos in the Pictures library and still keep the folder on your Desktop for ready access.

Libraries are particularly vital in Windows 8 since a lot of the applications on the Start screen such as Photos, Music and Vides use the libraries in looking for and displaying their content. For instance, all of the photos in your Pictures library are also in your Photos app.

You need to note that the applications on your Start screen are optimized for media so that it will be more trouble-free for you to watch videos, listen to music and view your pictures. The File Explorer is an essential tool in organizing your current media files into libraries so that you can easily enjoy them right from your Start screen.

The My Music, My Documents folders and other certain folders are automatically included in their own applicable libraries. But you can add your own folders to any of the Libraries by first locating the Folder you want to add and then right-clicking on it. Choose the Include in library and then choose your preferred library. This technique allows your folder to be both in your library and in its original location.

Chapter 5: How to Get Started with the Desktop

The Start screen really is a cool new feature of Windows 8. But if you will be doing more than surfing the internet, watching videos and listening to music, you need to familiarize yourself with the different features in the Desktop view.

How to Work with Files

The details of the File Explorer were already discussed in the previous chapter. In this chapter, you will learn how to open and delete files, navigate through the various folders, and more.

After you have opened the File Explorer and you instantly see the document that you wish to open, you can simply double-click on it to open it. But if you still need to go through the different folders, the Navigation pane is very useful in choosing a different folder or location.

How to Delete Files

You can delete a file by clicking, holding and dragging the file directly to the Recycle Bin icon found on the Desktop. An easier way is choosing the file that you want to delete and then pressing the Delete key. Do not worry if you have unintentionally deleted a file. You can access the Recycle Bin to locate the deleted file and restore it to its original folder. You can do this by right-clicking the file that you want to restore and then choosing Restore.

But if you are certain that all files in the Recycle Bin can be permanently deleted, you can clear it by right-clicking the Recycle Bin icon and then choosing Empty Recycle bin.

How to Open an Application on the Desktop

You can do this by either clicking the application icon found on the taskbar or double-clicking the application shortcut found on the Desktop.

How to Pin Applications to the Taskbar

By default, only selected application icons will be included on your taskbar. But you can pin your most used application on the taskbar so you can readily access them. You can do this by right-clicking anyplace on the Start screen. You will then see a menu at the bottom of your screen. Choose the All apps button to show the list of all your installed applications. Look for the application you want to pin and the right-click it and then choose Pin to taskbar. You need to note, though, that you cannot pin all applications to your taskbar. There are certain applications that are designed to be launched from the Start screen only like Calendar and Messaging. Thus, you can only pin them to the Start screen.

How to Use Desktop Effects

Multi-tasking and working with several windows have become easier with Windows 8 because of the various Desktop effects now available to you.

- You can use the Snap effect to quickly resize open windows. This is particularly useful when you are working with several windows simultaneously. You can use the Snap effect by clicking, holding and dragging a window to the right or the left until you see the cursor reach the edge of your screen. Release your mouse to snap the window into place. You can easily unsnap a window by clicking, dragging it down and then releasing your mouse.
- Use the Peek effect for viewing the open windows from your taskbar. You can do this by hovering your mouse over any app icon on the taskbar that you want to view. You will then see a thumbnail preview of all open windows. You can view the full-sized window of the application by hovering the mouse over the app in the thumbnail preview.

- Use the Shake feature for selecting a single window from a clutter of open windows and then minimizing the rest. You can do this by locating and selecting the window that you want to concentrate on. You can then gently shake the window back and forth to minimize the other open windows. When you shake the window once more, all of the windows that you minimized will get maximized again.

- The Flip feature is useful in scrolling across a preview of all your open windows. You can also view any of the open applications on your Start screen using the Flip preview. The first three features – Snap, Shake and Peek – are for use only on the Desktop view. The Flip feature, on the other hand, can be used similarly in both the Desktop view and the Start screen. You can access the Flip preview by pressing and holding the Alt key and then pressing the Tab key. While you are still pressing the Alt key, press the Tab key to continue scrolling through your open windows. When you have spotted the application or the window that you want to view, stop pressing the Alt and Tab keys to display the app or window.

Conclusion

Thank you again for purchasing this book!

I hope this book was able to help you to use the new features of Windows 8.

The next step is to start personalizing your own Windows 8 so you can get the most out of it.

Finally, if you enjoyed this book, please take the time to share your thoughts and post a review on Amazon. We do our best to reach out to readers and provide the best value we can. Your positive review will help us achieve that. It'd be greatly appreciated!

Thank you and good luck!

Book 2

Rails Programming Professional Made Easy

BY SAM KEY

Expert Rails Programming Success In A Day For Any Computer User!

Table Of Contents

Introduction 25
Chapter 1 Why Rails Matters 26
Chapter 2 Getting Started 28
Chapter 3Create Your First Project 30
Chapter 4 Say "Hello There!" 33
Chapter 5 Let's Do Something More 35
Chapter 6 Creating Article Title 37
Chapter 7 Creating the Form 38
Chapter 8 Save Your Data 41
Chapter 9 Make Your Articles Neat 43
Chapter 10 Create Some Rules, Too 45
Chapter 11 Update Articles 48
Chapter 12 Destroy Some Data 52
Conclusion 55
Check out My Other Books 56

Introduction

I want to thank you and congratulate you for purchasing the book, "insert book title here Professional Rails Programming Made Easy: Expert Rails Programming Success In A Day For Any Computer User!"

This book contains proven steps and strategies on how to learn the program Ruby on Rails and immediately create an application by applying the rudiments of this platform.

Rails is one of the newest and most popular platforms. Thanks to the growth of Internet, this platform has been targeting audiences that are quite interested in creating stable web designs. If your work involves the Internet and you want to implement ideas that would help you launch projects online, you would definitely want to learn how to code using this program. Within this book are everything that you need to learn from installing the platform, getting the basics and making sure that you are ready to rock any programmer's boat.

Thanks again for purchasing this book. I hope you enjoy it!

Chapter 1 Why Rails Matters

If you are a computer programmer, the Ruby on Rails platform would probably the next program that you have to learn how to use. It is also worth looking into if your work is largely based on design, and you want to try something current to make websites easy to manipulate and beautiful. It could also be the platform that would launch your career or create leverage for yourself at the office. Yes, this platform could be your trump card to your next promotion, or that awesome site that you have in mind.

What Rails Can Do For You

If you are wondering what good this program can do for most computer users, then here are the awesome things that you can get out of the platform.

1. Get to Code

Coding is not rocket science, and if you are using Ruby, you probably would not even feel that you are using a programming language. You would want to learn to code to retain what you are going to experience with the platform, so take the time to study anyway.

If you are getting into Rails, you do not need to be a Computer Science major. If you are a businessman who has a great idea for a web app and you want to try coding it yourself, then this platform may be your best bet.

2. Get to Code Better

Sometimes it is not about arguing what is the best platform out there and get drunk arguing which is the best among Python, Java, PHP, or Ruby. If you already know other programming languages, you would need to still keep up with the times and learn some new tricks. Ruby on Rails provides that opportunity.

3. Get to Code Faster

RoR is a beautiful platform that allows you to write shorter codes, and it has a great set of features for exception handling which makes it really easy to spot and handle possible errors. You also would not need to still maintain the usual reference counts in your extension libraries. You also get awesome support using Ruby from C, which gives you better handle when you want to write C extensions.

RoR makes any programmer productive because it is opinionated and it gives guesses on how you can probably code something in the best way possible. The Don't Repeat Yourself (DRY) Principle of RoR also makes you skip the usual coding process of writing something again and again, which often makes the code long, complex, and difficult to debug. That means that at the end of the project, you get to look at your code and have a better grasp of what happened there.

4. Understand How Twitter Works

Yes, Twitter is created using RoR, and if you are an SEO specialist, a web designer, or simply a tech geek, knowing how this social media platform is done would definitely help you out. You would also discover that a lot of the hot new websites today are built on this platform.

5. Learn a Platform with a Great Community

RoR is relatively young compared to other programming languages, and for that reason, it has a very active and collaborative community. You definitely would get to hang out with several other developers and would probably build something together. Doing that is always good for your résumé.

6. It works with all operating systems and offers threading that is independent from the operating system. That means that is also very portable, and would even work on a computer that runs on Windows 95.

If these perks sound great, then it's time to get started with a Rails project!

Chapter 2 Getting Started

If you want to learn how to use Rails, then you would need to first have the following:

1. Ruby – choose the language version that is 1.9.3, or later. You can download it by visiting ruby-lang.org.

2. RubyGems packaging system – it is typically installed with Ruby that has versions 1.9 or newer.

3. Installed SQLite3 Database

Rails, as you probably figured out, is a framework dedicated to web application development written in the language of Ruby. That means that you would want to learn a little bit of Ruby coding in order to eliminate any difficulty in jumping into Rails. If you have a browser open, you can get great help in practicing Ruby codes by logging in to tryruby.org, which features a great interactive web tutorial. Try it out first to get the hang out of coding with Ruby.

If you do not have any working SQLite 3 yet, you can find it at sqlite.org. You can also get installation instructions there.

Installing Rails

1. Run the Rails installer (for Windows and Mac users) or the Tokaido (Mac OS X users)

2. Check out the version of the installed Ruby on your computer by running the Run command on Start menu and then typing cmd on the prompt (Windows). If you are running on Mac OS X, launch Terminal.app.

Key in "$ ruby –v" (no captions). After you hit Enter, you will see the Ruby version installed

3. Check out the version of SQLite3 installed by typing "$ sqlite3 –version".

4. After Rails installation, type in "$ rails –version" on Terminal.app or at the command prompt. If it says something similar to Rails 4.2.0, then you are good to go.

A Note on the $ sign

The $ sign would be used here in this book to look like the terminal prompt where you would type your code after. If you are using Windows for the Rails platform, you would see something like this: c:\source_code> .

Chapter 3 Create Your First Project

Here's something that most web developers are raving about Rails: it comes with generators, or scripts that are made to make development a lot easier by making all things that you need to get started on a particular project. Among these scripts is the new application generator, which gives you the foundation you need for a new Rails app so you do not have to write one yourself. Now that allows you to jump right into your code!

Since you are most likely to build a website or an API (application program interface), you would want to start coding a blog application. To start, launch a terminal and go to any directory where you can create files. On the prompt, type "$ rails new blog."

After you hit Enter, Rails will start making an application called Blog in the directory. It will also start making gem dependencies that you already have in your Gemfile bundle install.

Now, go to where your blog app is by typing in "$ cd blog".

What's in There?

Once you get into the directory, you will find a number of files that Rails have already installed by default. If you are not quite sure about what these files are for, here's a quick rundown of the file or folder functions:

1. app/ - this has the models, helpers, mailers, assets, and controllers for the app you just created. You'll be looking more at this folder later.

2. bin/ - this has the script that you will use to run the app. Also, this has other scripts that you will be using to deploy, setup, or run the application you are going to create.

3. config/ - this allows you to tweak the app's database, routes, etc.

4. config.ru – this is the configuration that will be used by Rack-based servers to run the app.

5. db/ - this would contain your database and database migrations

6. Gemfile, Gemfile.lock – these would allow you to tell the program what sort of gem dependencies you are going to need for the app you're building.

7. lib/ - contains the extended modules needed for the app

8. lib – contains the app's log files

9. public/ – this would be the sole folder that other people could see. It would be containing all your compiled assets and created static files.

10. Rakefile – this would be the one file that would locate and load tasks that can be set to run from the command line. You can add tasks that you would prefer to use later on by adding the files needed to the lib/tasks directory

11. README.rdoc – just like readme's function, this would be a brief document that would tell other people how your app works, how to set it up, etc.

12. test/ - these would contain all your unit tests and all the things that you are going to need for testing.

13. tmp/ - this would hold all temporary files

14. vendor/ - this would contain all your third-party codes and would also contain all vendored gems.

Now, if you are seeing all these in the app directory you just made, then you are ready to create little bits and pieces that you would be adding up later to make a real blog app!

Firing Up the Web Server

Since you already have the barebones of your blog application, you would want to set up how the app is going to be launched on the internet. To start a web server go to the directory where blog is located, and then type "$ bin/rails server".

Important note:

You would need to have a JavaScript runtime available in your computer if you want to use asset compression for JavaScript or if you want to compile a CoffeeScript. Otherwise, you would expect to see an execjs error when you attempt to compile these assets. If you want to look at all the supported runtimes, you can go to github.com/sstephenson/execjs#readme.

If you are successful, what you just did would launch WEBrick, which is the server that Ruby apps use by default. You can see what's happening so far in your app by firing up a web browser and typing http://localhost:3000. Now, since you have done nothing much, you would be seeing the Rails default page. It will tell you that you are currently in development mode. You also do not need to constantly require the server to look at the changes that you have made – any changes will be automatically picked up and seen. Also keep in mind that if you managed to see this "Welcome Aboard" thing, you are sure that you created an app that is configured correctly. If you want to find out the app's environment, click on "About your application's environment" link.

Got everything right so far? Let's move on to making something other people can read.

Chapter 4 Say "Hello There!"

If you want to make Rails learn how to say Hi to other people, you would need the following:

1. A controller

The purpose of a controller is to allow your program to receive any requests. When you route, you enable Rails to decide which of the controllers you set up will receive which types of requests. That may also mean that there would be different routes leading to the controller, which would be triggered by specific actions. An action is required in order to collect any information needed in order to send it to a view

2. A view

This thing's main purpose is to enable Rails to display the information made available to the action and display it in a format that other people can read. There are different view templates that are already available and coded using eRuby, which can be used in request cycles before it the information is sent to anyone who wants to look at this information.

Got it? Good. Now, to setup your welcome page, you need to generate a controller and then name it "welcome" using an action named "index". Your code will look like this:

```
$ bin/rails generate controller welcome index
```

Now, Rails will be creating a bunch of files plus a route for you to use. When Rails is done with that, you will see this:

```
create  app/controllers/welcome_controller.rb
 route  get 'welcome/index'
invoke  erb
create    app/views/welcome
create    app/views/welcome/index.html.erb
invoke  test_unit
create    test/controllers/welcome_controller_test.rb
invoke  helper
create    app/helpers/welcome_helper.rb
```

```
invoke  assets
invoke   coffee
create    app/assets/javascripts/welcome.js.coffee
invoke   scss
create    app/assets/stylesheets/welcome.css.scss
```

If you want to view where the course of your controller is, go to app/controllers/welcome_controller.rb. If you want to look at the view, you can find it at app/views/welcome/index.html.erb.

Here comes the fun part. Pull up a text editor and open app/views/welcome/index.html.erb there. Clear all the codes you see there, and replace it with this:

```
<h1>Hello Rails!</h1>
```

After doing so, you have successfully informed Rails that you want "Hello Rails!" to appear. That means that it is also the greeting that you want to see when you go to http://localhost:3000, which is still displaying "Welcome aboard".

Create the App's Home Page

The next thing that you need to do is to tell Rails where the home page is. To do that, pull up your text editor again and open config/routes.rb. You should see something like this:

```
    Rails.application.routes.draw do
get 'welcome/index'

# The priority is based upon order of creation:
# first created -> highest priority.
#
# You can have the root of your site routed with "root"
# root 'welcome#index'
#
# ...
```

Those lines represent the routing file which tells Rails how to link requests to specific actions and controllers. Now, find the line "root 'welcome#index'" and uncomment it. When you get back to http://localhost:3000, you will see that it now displays Hello Rails!

Chapter 5 Let's Do Something More

Now that you have figured out how to make a controller, a view, and an action, it's time to create a new resource. A resource is something that groups together similar objects the same way you group people, plants, and animals. To make items for resources, you use the CRUD method (create, read, update, destroy).

Rails make it easy for you to build websites because it already comes with a method for resources that it can use for making a REST resource. REST, or Representational State Transfer is known as the web's architectural structure which is used to design all applications that use a network, and instead of using rather complex operations to link two machines, you can use HTTP to make machines communicate. That means that in a lot of ways, the Internet is based on a RESTful design.

Now, following the project you are creating, pull up config/routes.rb and make sure it's going to look like this:

```
Rails.application.routes.draw do

  resources :articles

  root 'welcome#index'
end
```

If you are going to look at the rake routes, you will notice that Rails has already made routes for all actions involving REST. It is going to look like this:

```
$ bin/rake routes
      Prefix Verb   URI Pattern                  Controller#Action
    articles GET    /articles(.:format)          articles#index
             POST   /articles(.:format)          articles#create
 new_article GET    /articles/new(.:format)      articles#new
edit_article GET    /articles/:id/edit(.:format) articles#edit
     article GET    /articles/:id(.:format)      articles#show
             PATCH  /articles/:id(.:format)      articles#update
             PUT    /articles/:id(.:format)      articles#update
             DELETE /articles/:id(.:format)      articles#destroy
```

root GET   /   welcome#index

Chaper 6 Creating Article Title

This part would be the creating and reading part of CRUD, where you would put in a location where you would be placing articles for the blog you're building. In order to do so, you can create an ArticlesController by running this code:

```
$ bin/rails g controller articles
```

Now, you need to manually place an action inside the controller that you just created. Go to app/controllers/articles_controller.rb and pull up the class ArticlesController. Edit it to look like this:

```
class ArticlesController < ApplicationController

  def new

  end

end
```

You now have to create a template that Rails would be able to view. In order to create a title for the article that you want to display, pull up app/views/articles/new.html.erb and make a new file there. Type the following:

```
<h1>New Article</h1>
```

What did just happen? Check out http://localhost:3000/articles/new and you will see that the page now has a title! You will now want to create a template that will look like a form that you can fill up to write your articles in online.

Chapter 7 Creating the Form

Pull up app/views/articles/new.html.erb and then add this code:

```
<%= form_for :article do |f| %>
  <p>
    <%= f.label :title %><br>
    <%= f.text_field :title %>
  </p>

  <p>
    <%= f.label :text %><br>
    <%= f.text_area :text %>
  </p>

  <p>
    <%= f.submit %>
  </p>
<% end %>
```

You will see that you have just created a form that has a space for the article title text, submit button, and it comes with boxes too! That is the function of the code form_for. You will realize that when you submit an article you are going to create, it needs to be done in another URL and then the entire text should then go somewhere else. Edit app/views/articles/new.html.erb by finding the form_for line and make it look like this:

```
<%= form_for :article, url: articles_path do |f| %>
```

In Rails, the action "create" does the job of making new forms for submissions, and therefore, your form should be working towards this action. You would notice that when you try to submit an article, you would see an error there. In order to make it work, you need to make a "create action" within the ArticlesController.

Create the Article

In order to get rid of this error, you need to edit the ArticlesController class found in app/controllers/articles_controller.rb. It should look like this:

```
class ArticlesController < ApplicationController
    def new
    end

    def create
    end
end
```

Once that is done, the controller should now be able to save the article to the database. Now, you would need to set the parameters of actions done by controllers. Now, make the ending of the above lines to look like this instead:

```
    def create
      render plain: params[:article].inspect
    end
```

Now that should make the error go away. Try refreshing the page to see what happened.

Make the Model

Rails already provide a generator that would be used by your project to launch a model. To order Rails to start generating one, run this on the terminal:

```
$ bin/rails generate model Article title:string text:text
```

What just happened is that you told Rails that you are requiring an Article model that has a title and a text that are attributed to separate strings. You would see that the platform made up a lot of files, but you would be most interested in db/migrate/20140120191729_create_articles.rb which contains your blog's database.

Now, you would want to run a migration, which you can do with a single line of code:

```
$ bin/rake db:migrate
```

What Rails would do is that it would be executing this command which means that it made the Articles Table:

```
== CreateArticles: migrating ===========================================
-- create_table(:articles)
  -> 0.0019s
== CreateArticles: migrated (0.0020s) ==================================
```

Chapter 8 Save Your Data

Pull up app/controllers/articles_controller.rb and edit the "create" action into this:

```
def create
  @article = Article.new(params[:article])

  @article.save
  redirect_to @article
end
```

You're almost able to create an article! However, when you refresh the page, you would see a Forbidden Attributes Error, and would point you at the line @article – Article.new(params[:article]). The reason Rails is giving you a hard time is because it wants you to tell what parameters should be in your controller actions. That allows your program to be secure once you run it, and prevent it from assigning wrong controller parameters which can make your entire coded program crash.

To fix this, edit out the highlighted line in the error you just saw and change it into:

```
@article = Article.new(params.require(:article).permit(:title, :text))
```

Show Your Work

In order to make the page display your article, you can make use of the "show" action by adding it to app/controllers/articles_controller.rb. Add these following lines:

```
class ArticlesController < ApplicationController
  def show
    @article = Article.find(params[:id])
  end

  def new
  end
```

Now let's add some style. Create a new file named app/views/articles/show.html.erb and put in the following lines:

```
<p>
 <strong>Title:</strong>
 <%= @article.title %>
</p>

<p>
 <strong>Text:</strong>
 <%= @article.text %>
</p>
```

Refresh http://localhost:3000/articles/new and then you will see that you can create articles and display them!

Chapter 9 Make Your Articles Neat

Find a way to list all the articles that you are going to create in order to have an organized database. To do that, pull up app/controllers/articles_controller.rb and add the following lines to create a control.

```
class ArticlesController < ApplicationController
 def index
  @articles = Article.all
 end

 def show
  @article = Article.find(params[:id])
 end

 def new
 end
```

Now, to add a view, pull up app/views/articles/index.html.erb and then add the following lines:

```
<h1>Article List</h1>

<table>
 <tr>
  <th>Title</th>
  <th>Text</th>
 </tr>

 <% @articles.each do |article| %>
  <tr>
   <td><%= article.title %></td>
   <td><%= article.text %></td>
  </tr>
 <% end %>
</table>
```

Head over to http://localhost:3000/articles and you will see all the articles that you have made so far.

Tidy Up Some More with Links

You definitely need to create links for the articles that you have created so your readers can pull them up easily. To add links, open app/views/welcome/index.html.erb and then change it to look like this:

```
<h1>Hello, Rails!</h1>
<%= link_to 'My Blog', controller: 'articles' %>
```

Now, what if you want to add a link that would allow you to write a new article right away? All you need to do is to add the following lines to app/views/articles/index.html.erb to have a New Article link:

```
%= link_to 'New article', new_article_path %>
```

If you want to create a link to go back to where you were previously, add the following lines to the same file:

```
<%= form_for :article, url: articles_path do |f| %>
 ...
<% end %>

<%= link_to 'Back', articles_path %>
```

Chapter 10 Create Some Rules, Too

When you are creating a blog program, you do not want your users to accidentally submit a blank page, and then just land right back where they were without knowing what they did. Rails can help you make sure that doesn't happen by editing the app/models/article.rb file to look like this:

```
class Article < ActiveRecord::Base
  validates :title, presence: true,
            length: { minimum: 5 }
end
```

That means that the title should be at least 5 characters in order for the article to go through, otherwise it would not be saved. Now that this rule for your blog is in place, you need to show the blog user that something went wrong and that the form should be filled up properly. To do that, tweak the "create" and "new" actions in app/controllers/articles_controller.rb in order to look like this:

```
def new
  @article = Article.new
end

def create
  @article = Article.new(article_params)

  if @article.save
    redirect_to @article
  else
    render 'new'
  end
end

private
  def article_params
    params.require(:article).permit(:title, :text)
  end
```

What just happened is that you told Rails that if the user did not type in 5 characters in the Title field, it should show the blank form again to the user. That doesn't offer much help. In order to tell the user what went wrong, edit the app/controllers/articles_controller.rb file again and to cater the following changes:

```
def create
  @article = Article.new(article_params)

  if @article.save
    redirect_to @article
  else
    render 'new'
  end
end

def update
  @article = Article.find(params[:id])

  if @article.update(article_params)
    redirect_to @article
  else
    render 'edit'
  end
end

private
  def article_params
    params.require(:article).permit(:title, :text)
  end
```

Now, to show this to the user, tweak the app/views/articles/index.html.erb file and add the following lines:

```
<table>
  <tr>
    <th>Title</th>
    <th>Text</th>
    <th colspan="2"></th>
  </tr>
```

```
  <% @articles.each do |article| %>
    <tr>
      <td><%= article.title %></td>
      <td><%= article.text %></td>
      <td><%= link_to 'Show', article_path(article) %></td>
      <td><%= link_to 'Edit', edit_article_path(article) %></td>
    </tr>
  <% end %>
</table>
```

Chapter 11 Update Articles

You would expect your users to change their minds about the article that they just wrote and make some changes. This would involve the Update action in CRUD, which would prompt you to add an edit action in the ArticlesController and add this function between the "create" and "new" actions. It should look like this:

```
def new
  @article = Article.new
end

def edit
  @article = Article.find(params[:id])
end

def create
  @article = Article.new(article_params)

  if @article.save
    redirect_to @article
  else
    render 'new'
  end
end
```

To allow a view for this, create a file and name it app/views/articles/edit.html.erb and then put in the following lines:

```
<h1>Editing article</h1>

<%= form_for :article, url: article_path(@article), method:
:patch do |f| %>

  <% if @article.errors.any? %>
   <div id="error_explanation">
    <h2>
     <%= pluralize(@article.errors.count, "error") %>
prohibited
```

```
      this article from being saved:
    </h2>
    <ul>
      <% @article.errors.full_messages.each do |msg| %>
        <li><%= msg %></li>
      <% end %>
    </ul>
  </div>
<% end %>

<p>
  <%= f.label :title %><br>
  <%= f.text_field :title %>
</p>

<p>
  <%= f.label :text %><br>
  <%= f.text_area :text %>
</p>

<p>
  <%= f.submit %>
</p>

<% end %>

<%= link_to 'Back', articles_path %>
```

Now, you would need to create the “update” action in app/controllers/articles_controller.rb. Edit the file to look like this:

```
def create
  @article = Article.new(article_params)

  if @article.save
    redirect_to @article
  else
    render 'new'
  end
end
```

```
def update
  @article = Article.find(params[:id])

  if @article.update(article_params)
    redirect_to @article
  else
    render 'edit'
  end
end

private
  def article_params
    params.require(:article).permit(:title, :text)
  end
```

In order to show a link for Edit, you can edit app/views/articles/index.html.erb to make the link appear after the Show link.

```
<table>
  <tr>
    <th>Title</th>
    <th>Text</th>
    <th colspan="2"></th>
  </tr>

  <% @articles.each do |article| %>
    <tr>
      <td><%= article.title %></td>
      <td><%= article.text %></td>
      <td><%= link_to 'Show', article_path(article) %></td>
      <td><%= link_to 'Edit', edit_article_path(article) %></td>
    </tr>
  <% end %>
</table>
```

Now, to give chance for the user to Edit his work, add these lines to the template app/views/articles/show.html.erb:

```
...
```

```
<%= link_to 'Back', articles_path %> |
<%= link_to 'Edit', edit_article_path(@article) %>
```

Chapter 12 Destroy Some Data

No, it does not mean that you have to ruin the entire program you built. At this point, you would need to make provisions for the user to delete some of the articles that he wrote. Since you are creating a RESTful program, you would need to use the following route:

```
DELETE /articles/:id(.:format)     articles#destroy
```

This route makes it easy for Rails to destroy resources and you would need to make sure that it is placed before the protected or private methods. Let's add this action to the app/controllers/articles_controller.rb file:

```
def destroy
  @article = Article.find(params[:id])
  @article.destroy

  redirect_to articles_path
end
```

After doing so, you would notice that the ArticlesController in app/controllers/articles_controller.rb will now appear this way:

```
class ArticlesController < ApplicationController
  def index
    @articles = Article.all
  end

  def show
    @article = Article.find(params[:id])
  end

  def new
    @article = Article.new
  end

  def edit
    @article = Article.find(params[:id])
```

```
end

def create
  @article = Article.new(article_params)

  if @article.save
    redirect_to @article
  else
    render 'new'
  end
end

def update
  @article = Article.find(params[:id])

  if @article.update(article_params)
    redirect_to @article
  else
    render 'edit'
  end
end

def destroy
  @article = Article.find(params[:id])
  @article.destroy

  redirect_to articles_path
end

private
  def article_params
    params.require(:article).permit(:title, :text)
  end
end
```

Now, it's time for you to let the user know that they have this option. Pull up the app/views/articles/index.html.erb file and add the following lines:

```
<h1>Listing Articles</h1>
```

```
<%= link_to 'New article', new_article_path %>
<table>
 <tr>
  <th>Title</th>
  <th>Text</th>
  <th colspan="3"></th>
 </tr>

 <% @articles.each do |article| %>
  <tr>
   <td><%= article.title %></td>
   <td><%= article.text %></td>
   <td><%= link_to 'Show', article_path(article) %></td>
   <td><%= link_to 'Edit', edit_article_path(article) %></td>
   <td><%= link_to 'Delete', article_path(article),
        method: :delete,
        data: { confirm: 'Are you sure?' } %></td>
  </tr>
 <% end %>
</table>
```

You would notice that you also added up a feature to make the user confirm whether he really would want to delete the submitted article. Now, in order to make the confirmation box appear, you need to make sure that you have the file jquery_ujs in your machine.

Conclusion

Thank you again for purchasing this book!

I hope this book was able to help you to grasp the basics of Ruby on Rails and allow you to create a webpage based on the codes and processes discussed in this book.

The next step is to discover other applications of the platform and learn other Rails techniques that would improve your program design and integration.

Finally, if you enjoyed this book, please take the time to share your thoughts and post a review on Amazon. We do our best to reach out to readers and provide the best value we can. Your positive review will help us achieve that. It'd be greatly appreciated!

Thank you and good luck!

Check Out My Other Books

Below you'll find some of my other popular books that are popular on Amazon and Kindle as well. Simply click on the links below to check them out. Alternatively, you can visit my author page on Amazon to see other work done by me.

C Programming Success in a Day

Python Programming Success in a Day

PHP Programming Professional Made Easy

HTML Professional Programming Made Easy

CSS Programming Professional Made Easy

Windows 8 Tips for Beginners

C Programming Professional Made Easy

JavaScript Programming Made Easy

C ++ Programming Success in a Day

Programming Box Set #99: Windows 8 Tips for Beginners & Rails Programming Professional Made Easy

If the links do not work, for whatever reason, you can simply search for these titles on the Amazon website to find them.